I0223923

11781 W. Sunset Boulevard

Also by Simon Smith

North Star
LEXICON
Night Shift
Juicy Fruit
Fifteen Exits
Reverdy Road
Mercury
London Bridge
Gravesend

Simon Smith

11781 W. Sunset Boulevard

Shearsman Books

First published in the United Kingdom in 2014 by
Shearsman Books
50 Westons Hill Drive
Emersons Green
BRISTOL
BS16 7DF

Shearsman Books Ltd Registered Office
30–31 St. James Place, Mangotsfield, Bristol BS16 9JB
(this address not for correspondence)

www.shearsman.com

ISBN 978-1-84861-322-5

Copyright © Simon Smith, 2014.
The right of Simon Smith to be identified as the author
of this work has been asserted by him in accordance with the
Copyrights, Designs and Patents Act of 1988.
All rights reserved.

Acknowledgements
Some of these poems appeared in the following publications or were
published by the following publishers, sometimes in different versions
or in different forms:
FENCE, Molossus Magazine, OR, Shearsman,
Tears in the Fence, Veer Books, Zone.
Special thanks go to Stephen Mooney for his
enthusiasm in regard to the sequence, 'Gravesend', and to
Nick Bodimeade for his painting, sometimes a blob (2009).

Cover image, sometimes a blob
copyright © Nick Bodimeade, 2009.

Contents

11781 W. Sunset Boulevard

for Guy & Béatrice

Like earlier generations of English intellectuals who taught themselves Italian in order to read Dante in the original, I learned to drive in order to read Los Angeles in the original.
— Reyner Banham

A crazy little place called 'Be There Now'
— Steely Dan

The cars hiss by my window, like the waste down on the beach
—The Doors

Ode: Sat Nav Narrative on Flying into LAX

Hopping the Hudson Strait to Hudson
Bay hurry not toward
450 m.p.h. of ground speed dip down at
James Bay distance to LA 2513 miles local
time at present position 12.30 p.m.,
next the Great Lakes a lot of cloud down
there & not far away the flight path
curves to the pleasing earth's curve,
eyes gritty-tired,
doggèd, filled with the hours bursting
the grit full of hours & Newcastle
Brown, Stella, some other forms of beer unidentified, & Thunder
Bay, LA in 2188 miles, a curl
of hair for the book's pages a charm
keeps our place, & at 38,000 feet everything's made
to look smaller
& now onto Winnipeg
using the Spacepen David bought for me all those years
ago now we're nearly in space &
four hours to go,
thinking of David makes me switch
to local time at London 6.23 p.m. & dark—
cold no doubt the 777 held above
like a mobile

or lunar module

returning Apollo 13

the stratosphere silent & moving forever

those still strapped into their business class

like to lick lips glistening

Winnipeg our event horizon

patchwork of lakes leading-edge forming vapour

breathe in & *The Collected Poems*

of Paul Blackburn becomes

my favourite book & all is clear

a life abandoned to the High Plains

between Cheyenne & Laramie in minutes

then on to Mount Rushmore & the Devil's Tower

the Colorado River, the Hoover Dam & Mojave Desert

now in the blue sky above LA now

is the moment for change & everything shifts forward next

Credit Card Reader

The only reading worth knowing
step towards the people carrier
ready to meet & capture this World
a grainy figure picks out street angels
pimp or punter hard to tell behind the windshield,
when the cars growl past my window
as the lone power-tool suddenly shuts off,
the naturally benign climate to LA
full of freeways & car interiors
with fixtures hard enough to bang my head into,
granulated neighbourhoods
watch the housing projects from surveillance footage
palm & fig trees, the gated communities.
This is Rilke calling collect from Los Angeles.

10/22/11

My last shave, when? Wednesday?
No, Thursday, before take-off. Two days' growth.
My friend Guy bringing Robert Crosson across from the dead,
heroic, a fine task, sleek in those black
Seismicity Editions—*Day Books*...
with Gaddafi's execution, NATO enters its 'over watch period,'
& we can be glad of the minimal collateral damage
& no NATO or American casualties, the causality
of which means, *erce*, 'the most successful operation
of Modern Times,' the casual rhetoric of the robotic U.S. military,
relaxed for National Public Radio, informs you & me,
no doubt without tie & top button undone, in his 501s
closer 'To The People,' voice of one, who is one of us.

Hummingbird

Sat at the window tuned to Sunday traffic
where are the drivers rushing
to their limitless gods over limitless tarmac
LA defines the horizontal—no bar, no limit
no known impediment, the grid
Rilke searching streets & corners, passing
cars like the grind of sharpening knives

Chandler's 'The Little Sister'

Relax beside the pool, palms, Scots pine not
now but next
                    the magnolias, tankers,
muscle cars, the thirst & appetite
inexhaustible for 24-hour neon artificial
sun, LA as far West as it goes before
becoming East
                        again, heading towards
Santa Monica up Route 405
'the beach is three miles that way',
the cab driver jabbed his thumb left
& West.

Windshield

iPhone pointing west on Sunset
smog swirls up from the coast
the zombie convoy of Corvettes,
Camaros, Trans-Ams—a wave
sweeps over West Sunset Blvd
to the STOP sign, & my feet,
this long haul long hop deep
breath, crossing the concrete
the red hand held up, eight
seconds

Commute

home space   —>   work space
in-car time-space the distance
to the office with my name on it
'SIMON SMITH H-462-44'
something something vacant
lot something something
Garnett's photos of Lakewood living
space, 'pragmatic solutions
to the problems of shelter,'
like printed circuitry
a white Mustang ('66?) rolls up
Sunset from Santa Monica
& the beach, the traffic
rolls with it, sucked up on rollers

Los Angeles River

Untroubled by birdsong
a big nowhere, 200,000 or more
windshields shimmer leaping
salmon upstream of I-405
built by robots, driven by utility
the cops airborne & mobile,
Bell Huey & Vaughan Williams'
'Flos Campi' housed
in a thousand automobiles
drifting up Sunset string
& voices to a thousand
exact copies without interference,
the Statue of Liberty 125 years young
today in the comfort of eeef-eeemm

Eyewitness News

'President Obama visited West Sunset Boulevard
today,' good to know he has friends in the neighbourhood.
We slept through the motorcade & chopper patrol
at our bedroom window & mid-afternoon dusk—
blue, orange, mauve, dove grey, sun strong, shadows
black, the blue-print or printed circuit of a city
tell me we've entered a TV comedy, cop show,
LA film noir, news bulletin, porn or snuff movie,
call me on 1 310 440 8323 when you know.

Brentwood

Writing the 'business' of Hollywood
the blue pool & blue, blue sky
politics laid down beside
the World stopped, all a-shimmer
drive up Wilshire you cross Euclid
grid not geometry to human
scale of break down into the drag
racer's day, trade in
my 501s for a *Pacific Standard Time*
catalog, five pea emm.
Sun strong then night. Dark, cold.
There is no climate in LA
there is no weather in San Diego,
flip the thermostat, chill, adjust.

Long Distance

Drive, & you take part, face life
face lift & the pure products
of the dream factory
we met at the intersection, drive
in, feel free, the printed circuit,
the 'lift' accept no
substitute, the elevator
a surgical procedure to capture
youth in face of the Other

An Email for David Herd: Anna's Hummingbird

Its flickering bright
                 body green then yellow then
one
        corporate environment
to the next
        red Camaro
flips lanes
        the hypodermic
bill, the Getty marble
-facings of High Modernism
air con on   I reach out   see
through   beyond   my thinking mid-sentence
                this grid of a notebook
the streets & drawn blinds   the boundaries
drawn down   capillary action   high above
the clouds like spaceships   boomerangs or flat-irons
the perimeter road   its razor-wire, dogs
you need a code—   zip, genetic, pin
a surgical strike on red
blossom   the Armed Response
of the Bel-Air Patrol   sucking up nectar
thru the epistemology of lime and lemon
Maseratis sip stamen to stamen   the cul-de-sac
               of show cars

on the beach @ Malibu

where your working day ends

mine begins, you can reach me

a new email address & Anna's Hummingbird

browsing for fructose   & walking is thinking not driving

a brace of pelicans flap across

11/1/11

Visit Paul in the reading room 'The New
Poetry Archive,' UCSD, visiting
Granpa at St. Liz's c.1950
EP's mad notes scrawled across tissue paper
in bold, broad lead pencil to the young
poet/translator of Provençal
two or three
hours spent marking up correspondence to xerox
Paul's a life
lived of job applications, resumés, bills
debts, love, business letters, Spanish/French trans-
lation, In. On. Or About. The Personal.
Close now, breath at my ear,
new as this minute gone

W. Pico

Cameras tree to tree
police the walkers & care
for our freedom the silver Elantra sedan
affords us, registration 5HFE080
on a California plate, hire
car dropping transmission oil
to the drive
tick tock tick tock tick tock
indicate, then veer to the left lane exit
up the up ramp, then down the down
flat slabs concrete sky
snug to concrete road the grey abandoned
buildings something something something
fits something to something & something

Hegelian Dialectics

$25,000 face-lift

non-stop on I-405

Paradise Cove

The last 'hello' of LA
before The East Terminal
Island, San Pedro
snaking out of W.
Sunset Blvd. The Pacific Coast Highway, then north north-west
along the coast
canyons inland lined up—Topanga, Corral,
Latigo, Ramirez,
where the miniature black Pomeranian goes surfing,
where the porno threesomes cruise—oh, cup
cake this ain't Proust's madeleine to bite into—
not even if you listen hard enough
release
the taste of almonds as Time drops below the sun
as human faces
run out of beach
bob below the surf no
recall sipping martinis or margaritas
Bourbon on ice down in Culver City
to loosen inhibition & tongue
the game
of Telephone down
the line re-surfaced as Chinese Whispers way out
East to play we're all free so long
as you follow the rules & we're 'Home at Last'

Out of Malibu

& Jim Rockford's Pontiac
cold case re-opened
Black Dahlia to the Zodiac Killer to Natalie Wood
a rainbow over LA
Downtown the pot
of gold & 14400 Sunset
Dennis Wilson's, see Manson slips
away the picture right, shadow
door to wall, & the singer stopped
breathing, surf boards propped
& golf courses manicured, we're neat
in line for chips &
soda, the return
to normal life & a be em double ya
chill to Chet Baker's
'The Thrill
is Gone'
looming with the rain
clouds over LA way too far
a city too big to fail
its up to the jury, you file your report back
to English money
the 747 tips around one eighty
out of the Pacific

the hundred Croydons of the west
& time before
the slip down across to Greenwich
the Meridian & one last 'hello' to LA
01:47 tomorrow from 17:47 today

Gravesend

for three men of Kent and Kentish Men,
David Herd, David Rees
and David Seabrook (i.m. 1960-2009)

'The air was dark above Gravesend, and farther back still seemed condensed into a mournful gloom, brooding motionless over the biggest, and the greatest, town on earth.'
—Joseph Conrad

'This is the winter of the mind.'
—The Fall

A Theory for a Materialist Poetics

I want my life to be a story once
Upon a time a four-legged now a three-legged rose
Wood table smashed along the railway cutting,
Its central leaf missing
As my eight-year-old collects climate-change transfers
Hungry for permanent structure,
A *Boost* bar and *We Love You* magazine.
The rag-man, a man made from rags,
Ticketing ideas, national and local
Initiatives added to the fun and sediment
By the lads in thick gloves and goggles:
Virgil and Horace lined up, but where's Martial?
Item by item dug under the fingernail,
Soft skills accompaniment to soft shells.
Sheppey clear through Canvey on a day
Like today's material never-ending list
Experience crammed in as far as the eye can see,
Surrounded by electric
Fencing blue air yellow sodium burns through
Acid-clear, the tough grasses cut like glass,
Where 'life' became a history to cry out
About grey and brown flatlands tilted
Over the edge dangling Pip.

Table of Contents

Quarantine Area a rhetorical question
When all hearts were broken
When all heart's stopped beating

Pegged together polyester blouse
Odd sock, panties, woollen skirt
Sour Candy, bramble, ivy, marram

Greenwich

Spangles' wrappers tumble along the north east coast
Hansel and Gretel hot on the trail,
But before we get into all of that:
'Welcome to Deptford'

History GCSE (Kent & Essex Board, June 2008)

'Is *anyone* going shopping?' The ascendant

Activity over and above questions of heritage

Or the role of collieries in the early 21st Century.

Question 1: '1984'

Where a half-brick to hand is worth

A throw through an open window comes in handy.

Police lined up aboard vans connive

Two knaves and three of a kind

Behind reinforced glass and grilles

Juvenal, Claudius, Caesar, heading west then north.

Maybe even Vespasian.

In the name of communications, or a tightening

Of political screws, any chance voted for

Representative to which words attach themselves,

Disease this side of the coastline

Progressive education, all the signs

Of liberal democracy and Neil Young's 'helpless,

Helpless, helpless' seeps from the bins, whilst 'The Sugar-

Plum Fairy' echoes its welcome about the estate,

Mr Whippy surrounded by mums and toddlers.

Norwegian container ship at anchor taking on units

Tight delicate little violets

Pinned to 'to do' lists

Read the landscape, read the form

And History is real

Gantry above a work yard

No movement on board

Drained of signs, the taxonomy holding

Dirt under the fingernail

First things first

Greenhithe for Bluewater

Assessment elides policing
May blooms in March
At the Monster Truck Derby it's the taking part
And sodium spots in my back yard

Milton Range

Alarm bells sound, then targets pop up a little
Above the heart, knock him dead
Marsh in front, heathland behind
Half-built conservatory ten years half-built
The Old English Sheep Dog—stuffed at Higham
Old toys out for the dummy run
Scouting for Baudelaires
Gen Star, Eurobulk, Accurate Roofing the next compound
To the next.
The boys with SLRs are gone, so who's to feed the animals?
For future reference pick up your *Observer Book of Wild Flowers*,
Sour Candy, bramble, ivy, marram
A few scraps to memorise genus.

Gravesend

Monday's coffee after Sunday's alcohol.
The land of rain and sodden trainers.
Body processes in the image. Freaks and dreck.
Countless body shops, Mondeos sent for scrap,
An odd Avenger, rust and 'sunburst copper'.
So this is where the scaffolders live recycling time,
And my credit's good, though I could raise the capital
Where the eyes can't look up and off
The blue miles putting the hours in.
It's fifty minutes from the Royal Marines Reserve,
Then past the incinerator.
There's a 'unit' to let out there,
A station to hang a place off
The girl with ankles snappy as couch grass,
The woman with no hair, a laughing dad to add,
Count off the stops
Two trucks stacked, Albatross
Removals, piles of motors tilted towards Medway.
'As the camera records our likeness
Without returning our gaze,' I make for the office and coffee.

Abbey Wood

Slade Green Depot Control Room
Is now declared out of it—the loop, control, *whatever...*
Wife-beater in paw, he's alright, he's okay
Just time for a sit down. It's early days yet
For Wat Tyler, for footfall and exercise
In community policing or prosody
(The wine better than hash).
Map to the Big City, looming behind your head
Feet straight out, Strood the other side

Questions of Communication

If you've got a radio, what kind of information do you send? It's what's handy.

Dartford

Silver shoes and derricks, the road to Temple Hill
Up, bearing left past the sun to 'I write this down
While I'm still in control'—Paul Weller.
The grey bin labelled 'not working' I mis-read for 'networking'.
The world's plastic floats its way to Midway.
So this is where all the broken toys go
The axe poised above the victim.
True to the digital, the Real under construction.
This is Dartford. This is Dartford. Heed the warning.

Allegro Equipe

Awarded the double: worst car ever built or designed.
A pile of them stacked between marsh and shoreline
Pre-date the internet or the mobile
You'll still need a licence, not qualified for vintage status
You'll need full insurance. Group F.

Cy Twombly

Say goodbye, Catullus to the shores of Asia Minor

Fun

Fun peters out at 45, so my body tells me
A skate-boarder and a guy with a stick,
Who will trip up who? Skate-boarding
Was never my *thang*, even back then.

Deposits

Refrigeration and containment
Not that far to the jail at Sheppey
Nationalise the debt for helicopter money
No time to think—extruded plexiglass,
Or a few details from my own personal experience
Is History in real time not sampled
The exchange of containers from ro-ros to lorries,
The male located in the female.

Tightrope

The coast winds up. Fetch your coat and stout shoes,
Build an armada, build an empire
Next to inflating the bouncy castle.
'General Gordon's Dude Ranch to re-open'.
Satchels off and reality occupies my slippers,
On the corner the man with the monkey
Is snapping snappy-snaps, Elephant
& Castle to The Empire samples
Off every continent up the road the main
Artery to the centre, Indian elephant,
Empress Diamond, Pocahontas—
Trophies, I'll be there but not back too late
To fall by the wayside to switch from analogue
To digital, switch to fictional from real. Whistle.

We don't stop at Deptford. No one dare.
Knife crime up 25%, red sails down river.
PVC harder wearing than diamonds,
Bet no chemist thought of that: use
Twenty minutes (twenty-five tops)—
Lasts a thousand years
Manufacture to landfill

Charlton

I'm sitting here taking notes
No one dare for long. We don't stop at Woolwich Dockyard.
Tarpaulin surrounds the crime scene
Arc lamps don't mix with sodium.
Thirty-five miles of landfill, objects
Drained of meaning and function we move on
Simply to survive, they only move about
A draft strategy.
Bluewater permanent construction site of the mind,
Construction workers look like archaeologists.
Housing below the flood-plain
Tucked next to the Wickes Home Improvement Centre.
Cans of Red Bull come shimmering home
To roost amongst flowering broom, hawthorn and bramble.

London Bridge

Dancing naked in the streets on their way to Blake's 'Jerusalem',
We move on to survive, Paul Weller's *Illumination*,
'A heavy load of nothing', toddlers' shrieks for bass,
Mechanical station announcement for treble.

Narrow Gauge

A sewage works like a nuclear power-plant
Domed containment building, to contain… what?
Chalk quarries behind, facing north
A whole coast gone to brown field

Lewisham

The anodyne spin pass me
A quick squirt of air
Freshener restores Arcadia
Where caravans and Sweet Jesus Lives
A town plummets down a chalk cliff,
Church, row of shops, council estate
Falling, the lot into multicoloured polythene
Crates for ships, trucks and freight.
Benjamin's *Illuminations* folded
Into a knapsack
Somewhere along the route
Peeled back to Northfleet, a semibreve
Into the middle of nothing
And the memory of nobody.

Rochester

The 'Largest Secondhand Bookshop in England' is always shut.
'Expectations' pub next door puts on a good show.
H0/00, train stations in order.
Boys' toys. A decommissioned sub
Listing 30°
Starboard, bows up
The Medway and all the king's men
Around the bend, the genes of Henry VIII
Are strong, the land of clockwork populated
By bobbing heads from Clockwork Orange,
Number ones and skins cradle
The ruling class today's
Lesson in human geography,
South-east England, opportunity
Classed a number one heritage site
Platforms tidy, bins half-empty,
Then half-full

Idyll

Stepped terraces emerging from Dartford,
Read off the charge sheet.
What I loved about the Zeitgeist was when I lived there.
Translating the image into the Real, then dissolve.
From deduction to guesswork,
All rails lead to Gravesend
All roads to Thamesmead, creek,
Recycling plant, lorry depot.
Do we need to join the dots,
Then read off the pro-forma?
Out of necessity? Sheep between pylons,
Pocahontas floats on the aura
Buried under Thamesgate.
Paddle steamer (c.1901) on the stocks at Rochester,
Opposite Burger King the outline of a Roman temple.
Chalk escarpment peeled back to landfill,
Reculver shimmers beyond that that way.

A Little Cushion

Affluent to effluent, *All Mod Cons*.
'Yes' traded for 'yes'. M.O.D.
Brought up to eye level but no further than that.
Creatives buying the products of your labour
Brought up to eye level recognition or seconds
Gone, a lost halo here: a lost hero there. Almost lost. Then gone.

Pit Bull

Expectorate as someone's going to kick off before someone
Starts muttering. Proof you can build a garden wall in 36 hours.
Analyse footfall, then you grasp reality,
And a sing-song good morning to you is how it goes.
Off-duty soldiers attentive to M.O.R.,
'The girls watch the boys watch the girls'—no narrative.
Those shoes in beige.
Print off the feeling, dad-and-daughter-
'Together-at-last,' chimes *The Sun*.
Hello, I'm Mr Gooseberry,
Shift one foot to the other,
Braced for the sugar rush—
There are two of them, twins, takes two to make a scuffle.
Being the neutral, one supports the underdog.

Pub

Runs a line in car parking, three quid a pop.
Paisley shirt for your birthday. Top
Button done up. Tailed by psychopaths
Seen off by ideologues. Don't blink, stay alive
Privatised we crave our square of turf,
Red Tops choca with soccer.
Stood over, service revolver to the temple.
Drop your voice, patina rubbed away
All hours, all round the houses, all
Round the hours, sequins to squint.
Manilow, Andy Williams, Monro.
Outside for a smoke where mums deploy toddlers
To 'the very thought of you'. Meanwhile,
Gurney plots his 'great' escape from Dartford Asylum.

Poet

The identity fraud you don't own up to.

OR

A tutorial with your creative writing lecturer.

OR

Being invited to interview with your bank manager.

Those Were the Days

Thames water you drink out of and shit into.

How much do they give in the pawnshop for the lyre?

Two actions, the one gesture. Peep bow and fort-da, structures
      the day.

Lager in a Strongbow glass, the injustice and asymmetry

Of life, clearly meted out and metered.

No worries about God—we've gone

For the basic plan, as a family.

Working your patch there's enough on your plate.

No email, no trail, no comeback. Simple.

A fine gent in a suit. No trial, no return,

Build quality a question mark for feedback control.

Aftershave smells like turpentine.

Skills-based or knowledge-based economy?

Pints and darts. Mr Guppy leaps up, happy dog.

Subaru Impreza

And a safe pair of hands, curvature above the rim.
Parents in their Sunday best, rickshaw peddling north
Marbled bruise above the chorus of blood,
Locates the shadow where you were held.
Pick your suit: clubs, spades, hearts, diamonds.
Clubs' trumps. Queen of spades the black maria.
Knock off the edges, move back to Chatham
Aura above that and that above aura

Lupercalla

Take away or tune in, look out for wear
A queue this morning
Your eyes lit up like shop windows.
Pens, brushes, pencils, tools for the senses.
Writing a paragraph would be a start,
Black ink and soot. We all fade as snow.
'I need a husband' with no ironic comeback.
Tuesday with staff, Wednesday with none.

Existential Crisis

You walk into a bar and order a Coke.

Opposite Asda

'Is a sonnet a helicopter?' enquired the girl
Who couldn't speak past her teeth.
Sediment ticking, whilst politics suspended
Above the heels by steel wires upside
Down, like Mussolini, fingers inked black.
Dracula's blood, concentration paper-thin,
Parked memory, Miles Davis *On the Corner*.
Mobile Computer Repair Centre,
Meccano and crop science.
Is your PIN number such a good thing
When you project-manage your holiday?
Begun with a question, obviously straight
As a dye arrows to anti-personnel mines,
so end with one end to end.

Holiday Cottage Bookshelf

Ian McEwan, *The Innocent*

Perdita, Paula Byrne,

Francis Itani, *Deafening*

The American Boy, Andrew Taylor

Kathy Lette, *Alter Ego*

Teesside Villages and Countryside

First Aid Manual

The Shadow of the Wind, Carlos Ruiz Zafon

Gervaise Phinn, *The Other Side of the Dale*

The Sixth Wife, Suzannah Dunn

Tom Sharp, *Wilt in Nowhere*

Helen Fielding, *Bridget Jones's Diary*

Gervaise Phinn, *Over Hill and Dale*

Susan Fletcher, *Eve Green*

High Force

Cars in droves parked pretty.

Drivers wearing English Heritage socks. Red diamonds.

Little Chef's hanging off the A1 all the way up

Like a Denby mug-tree.

'The dirty city & the dirty country,'

Golden section *in situ* this 13th day of August

Tangled symmetry by the toe,

Roads leading to mimesis huff and puff

And Gori empties its empty pockets.

History doesn't repeat itself, people do

Waiting for the Arriva bus never to arrive.

Pignut, meadowsweet, selfheal,

Making sense of the footfall in the faint path.

Last push to Low Force.

Agitprop Prop Olympiad

Is debt in the rise of purchase inputs the answer?
'How many references are there to Catullus
In Spenser's shorter poems?' Medway wedding
The Thames at Chatham? A squad not a team,
And how many Irishmen does it take to write *The Faerie Queene*
Trapped behind an inhuman surface of Olympic gold
Directly proportional to GNP? Sweet Thames run
Softly, third semi-final, next leg, first past the red flag
Page-turner, cut off the Coke supply to the village post office,
       knowledge
In storage my odyssey the lyrical to the digital,
I like the idea of the minor in the shorter,
And pick out suitable suitors from the ID parade of hopefuls:
Then pick up the river-bus at Nine Elms
Where the eighteen references hang suspended.

Seaford Beach

A local delivery van drops off Vit-bee,
Camp Coffee, KP Peanuts,
Man-made beach at Seaford, pixellated waves,
Pin-pricked bathers.

Knowledge in storage
The face of a clown nodding through the cello suites.
Ferries and containers await clearance for Portsmouth Harbour,
Passenger jets stacking above, silk routes through Asia Minor.

Chatham

End of the line. Iambic pentameter.

The message is the text—*Image, Music*

Text. Built like a Mig-21.

'Security personnel patrol this station

24 hours a day', the sign for Chatham

Sways in the breeze to the tune of 'Tin

Soldier', and our deepest non-narrative selves.

The low penetration of low production values,

School, department or faculty follow the business model,

Words cut from the wreckage Mr Charles Dickens scrambled
about

The carriage pitched towards Staplehurst.

We pause in our bucket seats to eat buckets full

Of chips, supporting the occupying forces who stick it out.

Portishead's 'Western Eyes',

This evening's soundtrack—20th March 2008 'This mess

We're in'. Me in pin-sharp form,

The ring-pull moment of chance,

Reality a line right through.

Coach D

'All you had to know were the answers,' Ornette Coleman:
Should be an epigraph to this one, but it's not, nor this:
'Can a thought have the quality of glare,' Clark Coolidge.
500cl of Diamond White kicking in, 9.47 a.m.
What do you think? The oracle's comical?
Judge a man by the way he treats his dog?
The truth elements are texts: stick to the Haynes manual,
Then you know where you are, the grey areas of South-East
        London,
777, Airbus overhead, crank the Golden Section to rote.
Ghost landscapes slip the train window, the order of red buses
In the wrong lane at the wrong time
Robert Browning opposite the Sophocles Bakery,
A sports-bag disguises warming Semtex, any sports-bag.
The virtual biography will be tackled in the follow-up,
Alongside a cement mixer in lime green,
On the stroke of six take your pick, but pick right
The operatives had no idea either, no reason to

White 440

Mileage half-way to the moon
Flew down the passage to miss the doors at Chatham.
The fewer the marks on her the happier we are.
If you threw the words away they will bounce back throwing fists,
Bad karma, like the kamikaze; use duck or roof ladders
Knee or crawling boards: the pages go tick, tick, tick—
What needn't show up in the final report
Life like most things in life is there to doodle through though
Requires training to flip and flop,
And 'Sex Dwarf,' by Soft Cell for an '80s vibe.
How you start is how you mean to go on, read those cards,
Read the Tarot, charge cards and the charge.

www.ingramcontent.com/pod-product-compliance
Lightning Source LLC
Chambersburg PA
CBHW031933080426
42734CB00007B/664